A.P.R.V.

ARMORED PERSONAL RETIREMENT VEHICLE

How one retirement vehicle can protect your savings from most of the typical pitfalls threatening retirement plans today.

KEVIN GOODWIN

CONTENTS

DEDICATION

I dedicate this book to my father, Staff Sargent Clifford Edward Goodwin.

My father is an incredible man who taught me the meaning of service. He served in the United States Army, is a father of four children, and truly is an example to me of service, dedication, and commitment. I truly hope and pray that I do as good a job as he did in teaching my children the meaning and value of service.

When he left the armed forces, my father was a staff sergeant serving at Fort Belvoir with the military police. Having been raised in a military family, I understand firsthand the commitments, sacrifices, and tremendous service that members of our armed forces (as well as their families) give up for each and every citizen of this beautiful country. For that I salute you, and I thank you for your willingness, commitment, dedication, and service—each of which are qualities that I admire and was fortunate to learn from my father.

Thank you, Dad.

PROLOGUE

I truly believe that information and education are the most empowering things in this world. When you know enough to make a decision about something, you become empowered with the ability to take action and do something about it. When you are uninformed and uneducated, it is very difficult to make a sure commitment and decision.

Can you imagine signing up for the armed forces and being sent into combat without any training, without any clear objective, without any intel on who it is that you may encounter or what their defenses may be? Oh, and by the way, can you also imagine that you are on your own, with no means of communication for the duration of the mission?

Of course you can't! It would be a futile mission that you'd have no hope of completing with any type of tangible success. Yet many Americans do just that with their retirement plans. They sign up for their 401(k) plan simply because their employer offers it. They do not have a clearly defined target or goal for when they want to retire. Nor do they know how much money they will need during retirement. They do not have a defined path or plan of attack to get them to their objective; the majority of them received very little information during their enrollment process. They are ill-equipped, unarmed, uneducated, and ill-prepared to make decisions that will provide measurable, tangible results to help them reach their goal.

Knowledge is *empowering*! Knowing your options, understanding the path that you need to take, and setting the goal that you want to achieve is the start of the empowerment process. You need to consider when you want to retire and how much income you need each year in retirement. Once you know that, you'll have the target in your scope.

Now is the time to establish your plan of attack, using all the intel that you have available. You need to determine a path and a plan that will provide you with the protection you need. You also need to consider who can help you develop this plan and how it can work for any contingency. Lastly, you should determine where your Quick Reaction Force (QRF) is. A QRF is a team, or individual, that can move in and help you with options, assisting you should you get in trouble on the way to your primary target.

It is critical to determine all of these things now so that you can put together a retirement plan that will give you the ability to reach your goal inside of your retirement horizon.

My hope is that those who read this book will become informed, understand the principles discussed, and be empowered with the ability to make decisions—*big* decisions that will shape their financial future, enable them to create their own personal financial independence, and achieve their dreams.

CHAPTER 1

MISCONCEPTIONS

ABOUT MONEY

"Education takes you places. Accounting education opens the door to the world of accounting. Financial education opens the door to freedom." ~ Robert Kiyosaki

I would like to start by debunking some of the most common misconceptions that a lot of people have about money and how it works. Some of these misconceptions come from our parents, some from misinformation provided to us. No matter where we developed these ideas about money, it is time to correct them.

THE MILLION-DOLLAR MISCONCEPTION

Many people have the thought or impression, "If I could just save one million dollars when I go to retire, then I would be set for life." Well, the truth is that the number varies for everyone. And it depends on what your plans are for retirement. But let's just take a second here and look at exactly what the million-dollar retirement can get you.

Let's assume that you have $1,000,000 in an IRA, 401K, or other tax-deferred account. You want to live off just the interest every year, so you place the money in an account that earns 5 percent interest. Now you're able to take out $50,000 per year without touching the principle. But then the taxes come out because its tax deferred, so between state and federal, let's assume you pay 22 percent in taxes. That means you pay $11,000 in taxes every year. Now, there are two variables here that we are making assumptions on: the tax rate and the 5 percent distribution rate. I will discuss these later in the book. However, with these assumptions, after you have worked hard and saved a million dollars toward retirement, you get to live off of $39,000 per year. Based on today's standards, your million-dollar retirement nest egg has given you the ability to live just below the poverty level.

There are better plans for retirement income than a blind belief in saving up to a million dollars. As we get further into the book, you will see how you can properly plan for the type of retirement that you want to live.

"YOU DON'T LOSE IT UNLESS YOU TAKE IT OUT"

There have been a lot of interesting ways that market losses have been spun. The investment firms have really done a lot to try to make you feel like market losses really do not affect you and that you won't be harmed unless you make changes.

Let me make this as simple as I can for you: *a loss is a loss*. What they are referring to here is that if you were to own a stock worth $100 and the stock dropped in value to $70, they explain that as long as you do not sell it at $70, you did not lose anything. The loss is not realized unless you sell or liquidate the asset. In a way, they are right, but this is very misleading because a loss was incurred. So to say that you do not have a loss unless you sell is incorrect. The fact of the matter is that you lost the time that it took for that stock to return back to its original value. If within two years the value went back to $100, you lost the $30 in growth potential that you could have had if the stock value never went down in the first place.

The investment firms have been very good at rephrasing losses in the market in ways that sound less negative. Have you ever heard of the term *market correction*? What they are saying is that they knew it was too high in the first place, and this new lower value is really where we should have been the whole time. Then why in the prior month were they telling me how great my investments were doing and touting the huge returns during that period, when by this logic they knew that those returns were inaccurate and would be eliminated when the market "corrected" to its accurate level? I don't know about you, but there's something that doesn't fit here. You cannot tout your gains and say market losses are not bad at the same time. I appears to me that they are trying to have their cake, and eat it too.

Again, understand this simple principle: *a loss is a*

loss!

THE LIE OF AVERAGES

We have all heard of the Law of Averages. I would like to introduce you to what I call "The Lie of Averages." This is the friendly fire of your retirement plan. As a misleading measurement of performance, averages are given to you on every statement you open. As you review these statements, it is difficult to identify the damage that your investment may be experiencing. I call it *friendly fire* because your own financial company is the one providing you with this potentially misleading information.

Let me introduce you to this problem with an illustration that will be very simple to understand. Let's say that you have $10,000 in an account. You then lose 50 percent, so now your account value is $5,000, right? So far, the math here is very simple. The next year your investment rebounds by 50%. So you earned 50% on $5,000, which means you earned $2,500 that year. This gives you an account value of $7,500.00. But if we were to look at your average rate of return over that two-year period, it is 0 percent. So how can your account balance be down by $2,500 on a 0 percent rate of return? Enter the Lie of Averages.

Texas baseball legend Bobby Bragan once quipped, "You could stand with one foot in a fire and the other in an ice bucket and, according to the percentage people, you should be perfectly comfortable."[1]

The reason I want to make sure you understand this simple principle is that when you discuss average rates of returns, it can be *very* misleading. Anytime there is a loss, it does not average out correctly. Let's look quickly at the S&P over a ten-year period and see how the Lie of Averages works out.

Chart 1-A. Lie of Averages

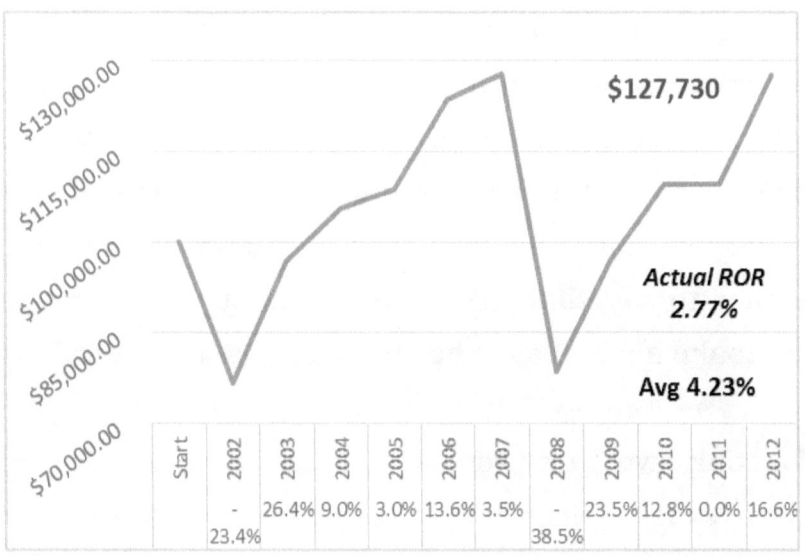

In the chart above, you can see that if we started with a value of $100,000 and ended ten years later, our account value would be $127,730. From this we could easily take the gains and divide by 10 years and then divide by the investment of $100,000 to see that our average rate of return is 2.77 percent. Now, if we take the annual rate of returns and average them out, you will get a 4.23 percent rate of return. That is an inaccurate representation of your actual returns.

Several years ago, there was an article in Forbes Magazine in which Investment Advisor David Loeper explained, "The investment industry standard of relying on time-weighted, compound return percentages as the principal tool for evaluating client portfolios and adviser performance has been a bad idea ever since it was adopted at the birth of the modern wealth management industry." He went further to say that "investment industry fuzzy math can make a client's losing year look like a winner." [2]

The only way to protect yourself from the Lie of Averages is to place your money in a place that *never* sees a loss. If you do not have a negative percentage, it cannot bring down your average rate of return.

THE TIME VALUE OF MONEY

While this may not be a misconception, I find that very few people truly understand the effect that time has on retirement. When we look at retirement, I typically talk about three different items that build wealth: time, rate of return, and money. Of these three, the one that has the greatest impact on your retirement is time. I wanted to take a few minutes to illustrate the effect of time on your money.

In the next table, Daron began saving at age 30 and saved $2000 per year for ten years. After the first ten years, he never put any additional money away. Madison started saving at age 40 and saved $2000 per year for 25 years. We will assume that both of them earned an annual interest rate of 8 percent every year. At the age of 65, Daron had only saved $20,000, and Madison had put away $52,000. Yet Daron would have $58,737.57 more money in his retirement account, than Madison.

Chart 1-B. Time Value of Money

Year	Daron's Contributions	Daron's Account	Madison's Contributions	Madison's Account Value
0	2000	2160		
1	2000	4492		
2	2000	7012		
3	2000	9733		
4	2000	12,671		
5	2000	15,845		
6	2000	19,273		
7	2000	22,975		
8	2000	26,973		
9	2000	31,290		
10	0.00	33,794	2000	2160
11	0.00	36,497	2000	4492
12	0.00	39,417	2000	7012
13	0.00	42,571	2000	9733
14	0.00	45,976	2000	12,671
15	0.00	49,654	2000	15,845
16	0.00	53,627	2000	19,273
17	0.00	57,917	2000	22,975
18	0.00	62,550	2000	26,973
19	0.00	67,554	2000	31,290
20	0.00	72,959	2000	35,954
21	0.00	78,796	2000	40,990
22	0.00	85,099	2000	46,429
23	0.00	91,907	2000	52,304
24	0.00	99,260	2000	58,648
25	0.00	107,201	2000	65,500
26	0.00	115,777	2000	72,900
27	0.00	125,039	2000	80,892
28	0.00	135,042	2000	89,523
29	0.00	145,845	2000	98,845
30	0.00	157,513	2000	108,913
31	0.00	170,114	2000	119,786
32	0.00	183,723	2000	131,529
33	0.00	198,421	2000	144,211
34	0.00	214,295	2000	157,908
35	0.00	231,439	2000	172,701
	$ 20,000		$ 52,000	$ (58,737)

The moral of the story: the sooner you start, the less you have to put away in order to get you to the same goal.

Start saving now.

NOT ALL INTEREST IS CREATED EQUAL: SIMPLE VS. COMPOUND INTEREST

You may have heard these terms before, but I want to define them and look at how the differences in interest can affect your retirement—especially if you are unaware.

Simple interest is interest earned on the principal balance only. If you have $1000 and earn 10 percent simple interest on your account, you will earn $100 in your first year. The next year you will earn the same $100. You will not earn interest on the interest in a simple interest account.

Compound interest lets you earn interest on all the funds in the account. When interest is earned, it gets applied to your balance, and you start earning interest on the new balance. The balance now reflects both the principal that you paid into the investment and the interest that you earned. In the same example of $1000 earning 10 percent interest, you earned the same $100 in year one. The difference here is that the next year you earn 10 percent on $1100, so you earned $110, and your new balance is $1210.

Because all interest is not created equal, you cannot compare a rate of return from one investment with another investment earning a different type of interest. Later in the book, we will talk about just how big a difference a compound interest account can make when compared to a simple interest account. But first, let's talk about what types of investments pay simple interest. Most people are unaware of the differences between these, how they can affect their accounts, and even what type of interest their investments are earning.

First, let's look at stocks. I will use the example laid out in chart 1-A. This is the perfect example of a stock-based account, and it will help you learn how to determine your rate of return. When you purchase a stock, you pay the current value of the stock. If you hold that stock for ten years and then sell the stock, you get paid the value of the stock at the time you sell it. So the stock's increase in value, if any, is what earns you money. You were not paid any type of interest each year, so no compounding would happen. This is a simple interest investment. In this example we can determine our simple interest rate of return by simply subtracting the principal from the current value. If you get a positive number, you earned money. If it is negative you experienced a loss on the stocks—in other words, you sold them for less money than you paid for them. Now we take the interest that you earned, $27,730, and divide it by the number of years that it took for you to earn that amount: $27,730/10 = $2,773. This is how much simple interest you earned each year. If we then divide that by the principal investment, it will give us our average simple interest rate of return: $2,773/$100,000 = .02773, or 2.773 percent.

Exchange Traded Funds (ETFs), most Government Bonds, Municipal Bonds, and Corporate Bonds, only earn simple interest.

One exception to the simple interest earned on

stocks is any stock that pays dividends—but only as long as those dividends are reinvested in additional stock purchases. Dividend payments on stocks provide you with a compounding effect. For example, mutual funds are managed funds in which a mutual fund manager manages the holdings. Typically, mutual funds allow the investor to elect automatic reinvestment of a fund's dividends into more shares of the fund. Because the dividends and growth are being reinvested into the fund, it creates a compounding interest rate. US Savings Bonds in the form of series EE and I bonds also earn a compounding rate of return.

HOW TO MEASURE SUCCESS

As you look at the different plans and options that you have available, I want to submit to you a simple proposition: you need to have a common measurement to compare the plans to each other. How can you compare one account to another without a common measurement by which to measure them? Do you look at how big the account grows to, your account balance at retirement, or your annual rate of return? We just talked about the Lie of Averages, so we know that we cannot use the average rate of returns as your yardstick. I would like to submit to you the following unit of measure by which to compare your options:

What plan puts the most money in your pocket each and every year, for the rest of your life?

When I put together retirement accounts, this is my primary focus; it should be your primary target! When you look at any other measurement, it really does not matter.

The interest rate can change, the taxes can vary, the growth may by simple or compound . . . there are so many different things to look at that can cloud your focus on what really matters. What really matters is how much money you get to live off of each and every year in retirement. Don't get caught up in the smoke and mirrors. Focus on what matters most to your retirement. The only things that matter are what you get to live off of without running out of money. If you measure every plan you look at with this same measurement, you will be amazed at what I am about to share with you. In fact, you will be shocked by how many advisors do not even talk about how much money you will have at retirement. They focus on other things to help you get there, but if they're not focusing on the goal, how are they going to help you accomplish it?

CHAPTER 2

INFLATION

Inflation is a battle that we will fight every single day. This is the relentless fire of life. I remember as a child I would often hear old-timers talk about "In my day," and then go on to explain how McDonald's Hamburgers were ten cents. And on and on they would go! My own father used to quip about how he would take five dollars and fill up his car for a run down to Los Angeles from his home in Atascadero. "At twenty-five cents per gallon!" he would exclaim. Well, as we all know, a gallon of gas is a lot more than that now.

What I find even more frightening is that even as I write this, I feel the years weighing on me. Just at the top of this paragraph, I referred to old-timers that used to talk about the prices back in the day. Well, I just had a realization that I must be one of those old-timers at this point. Many times I have explained to my own children how gas was 99¢ when I was in high school, and throughout this chapter, I will continue to discuss and show the dangers of inflation, all the while longing for the "Good old days."

Let me start be defining inflation for you:
Inflation, – noun: a general increase in prices and fall in the purchasing value of your money. [3]

I love this definition for inflation; it so clearly explains both hazards that we face from one single principle. Inflation not only raises the cost of everyday items but in so doing decreases the value of your dollar.

So let's look at how inflation can work against us in our retirement. This one can be very simply illustrated, but sometimes the impact may not be completely realized.

When we are saving money, we need it to grow so that we can live off of it during retirement. Most people do not and cannot afford to save 50 percent of their income. Yet inflation is working against us even as we save, eroding away at the purchasing power of our savings. So we need our savings to grow even faster in order to overcome that loss of purchasing power.

If your retirement account is barely keeping up with inflation, then it is not growing. While the account value may be increasing, if it is not beating the inflation rate, then by purchasing power, you're in the negative.

Inflation can be measured by the Consumer Price Indexes (CPI) program, which is administered by the US Bureau of Labor Statistics. It produces monthly data on changes in the prices paid by urban consumers for a representative basket of goods and services.

The change in the CPI is an accurate measure of the inflation rate. To make this very simple to understand, you can think of it like this: if you earned 8 percent on your investment, you could subtract the CPI's inflation rate (assume 3 percent) for the same period. This would give you the inflation-adjusted rate of return on your investment. In this example, that rate would be 5 percent. The average inflation rate from 2000–2009 was 2.29 percent, and the average over the last century was 3.22 percent. Further on in the book, when we discuss the solution to the problem of inflation, I will explain further how inflation can affect your retirement—not just during the accumulation phase but also during the distribution phase.

THE RULE OF 72

Let me use an example to teach you a principle that is extremely powerful for being such a simple equation. The rule of 72 simply states that if you take the number 72 and divide it by whatever interest rate you are earning, the result will tell you how long it will take your money to double based on a compound interest rate.

For example, if I am earning 4 percent compound interest in a CD or money market account, where the interest is credited every year, it will take 18 years for my money to double because $72/4 = 18$.

If I were earning 1 percent, it would take 72 years to double. Now, granted, 72 years is 28 years faster than it would take if it were in a simple interest account, but you can see the problem. Checking accounts now a days are paying .0125 percent interest (which would take 5,760 years to double!)

and the rate of inflation is over 2 percent.

And as a result of the losses in the market in 2007 and 2008, many people are not comfortable placing their retirement in the market. Instead, they are relying on banks, CDs, credit unions, and money market accounts, which are struggling to just keep up with inflation.

Since we now know how important it is to make sure that our money is growing enough to not only keep up with but to conquer inflation, let's discuss the options that we have to earn interest. To illustrate just how important it is to get a good interest rate, let's apply the rule of 72 to the next comparison.

If you are earning 4 percent from a money market or investment account, your money will double every 18 years. So let's assume that you have $10,000 in an IRA earning 4 percent and you are 29 years old. In 18 years, that money will double to $20,000, and in another 18 years it will double again to $40,000. By then you're 65 years old and ready to retire. You have $40,000 to your name. How long is that going to last you? A year, maybe? And that is just getting by—clipping coupons. Certainly not enjoying your retirement! Well, if you didn't have any more time and you didn't have any more money, the only other thing you could change would be the interest rate. Now, the big question here is, if you could have gotten a 10–12 percent interest rate, would that have made a difference? And the answer is absolutely! Let's take the same scenario but this time assume you're earning a 12 percent interest rate. Now, the rule of 72 says that if we are earning 12 percent, our money will double every six years (72/12 = 6). Now your money will double six times in the same 36-year period. So your growth would look something like this:

$10,000 (age 29)

$20,000 (age 35)

$40,000 (age 41)

$80,000 (age 47)

$160,000 (age 53)

$320,000 (age 59)

$640,000 (age 65)

That's right, $640,000! Same amount of money invested, same amount of time, but it cost the first guy $600,000 because he did not understand the interest rate principle. Now that looks like a pretty important principal to learn, right? Absolutely—it will change the quality of your life!

So where can you put your money so that it earns a high rate of return while providing you with protection form potential loss? There are three different places.

The first is known as a fixed investment. *Fixed* means simply that you earn the same predetermined rate of return every year. The problem with this scenario is that while we know exactly what we will earn, historically that return rate has been somewhere around 2–4 percent. And as we have discussed, a return rate of only 2–4- percent% does not allow our money to grow; it keeps us just treading water with inflation. The reason people like these investments are for the guarantee: you know that your money will be there when you come back.

Often, people look at this type of account and think, "Well, this way I can calculate and know exactly what I will have in my account in twenty years." The problem with this idea is that with most fixed accounts at banks, money market accounts, and CDs, the "fixed" rates can vary from year to year. So you do not have the ability to know exactly what you will have in your account 20 or 30 years down the road. In fact, very few fixed accounts actually guarantee the fixed rate for the lifetime of the account.

I cannot stress strongly enough the importance of beating the inflation rate. And fixed accounts can't beat it. They may keep up with it, but they cannot *win* the inflation battle.

Now you see the obstacle that people face in trying to grow their money. And this moves people in the direction of saving their money in the stock market.

In just a couple of chapters, I will show you how the Armored Personal Retirement Vehicle (APRV) will give you an option that allows you to earn a minimum fixed rate of return for the entire time you have the account, yet also gives you the opportunity to get an even better rate of return, while providing you the same guarantees.

CHAPTER 3

INVESTMENT LOSS AND RISK

The second way to earn interest is in the stock market and other variable-return investments. Throughout this book I will use the term "stock market," but understand that there are many different investments that work in a similar way, and for simplicity I will refer to them as the market.

The benefit that we have in the market is the ability to earn a large return on our investment. There are times that you will be able to see a 20 or 25 percent rate of return in a single year. This can be very exciting, but understand that in these investments where there is a high opportunity for reward, there is a correspondingly high potential for loss. You can lose your money just as fast as you earn it. In fact, the average investor lost 38 percent of their retirement savings in the fall of the market in 2007–2008. Many of those investors had to wait four or five years just to get their accounts back to where they were prior to the loss.

Now, I do not want you to think that I don't believe in putting money in these types of investments; they do have their place. What I have found in my experience is that too many people invest in the wrong direction. They get a job, go to work, and are told to start saving. The company offers a 401(k), so they do what they are being told to do and start investing in their 401(k), which is in the market. They blindly follow all the other people that believe that since this is what everyone else is doing, this must be what we are supposed to do. Understand that 93 percent of Americans[4] did not fail to retire at 65 because they did not try; they failed because they did what everyone else was doing! Everyone (statistically, almost everyone) is failing to hit their retirement goals—they don't have the ability to stop working at 65. And as we have been going through these issues, you probably see why: they have not taken the time to understand these issues, let alone find a way to avoid them.

So they start out saving for retirement and unknowingly become investors. They do not have a short-term savings account, and they do not have anything invested in a place that can give them some guarantees. They went straight to putting their money in a place that has a huge potential for loss. Some of them are even completely unaware of the position they are in. That is, until they start getting statements that show that they are losing money. This is, of course, assuming that they look at their statements at all. And you would be amazed at the number of people that I have met with that do not look at their statements.

People don't look at their statements for several reasons. The most common is that they do not know how to read the statement. It is very confusing. Sometimes they look at the before and after—the beginning-of-statement value and the end-of-statement value. If the second one's higher, then they're doing well, right? Not necessarily! If your beginning statement value was $32,000 and your end statement value was $34,000, you might think you did alright. But what about the $1000 per month that went into the plan over the last three months? If you had gotten a 0% return, your value should be

$35,000, so you actually lost more than a thousand dollars—but at first glance, the statement may make it look like you're doing just fine. This is just another of the hazards of the market: the hazard of not knowing or not understanding what your investment is doing and whether you are on track.

There is a time and a place for investing in mutual funds and stocks. However, far too many people that should not be in the market at all are there, and they are completely unaware of what they are doing.

I have talked in several places in this book about different reasons that the market investments may not work for you. The Lie of Averages; simple vs compound interest; misunderstandings and misinformation about loss; complexities of statements; and will soon address, the fees in the investment.

One of my favorite quotes that I learned as a child is this:

"Knowing is half the battle" ~ G.I. Joe

The issue I have with the market is that far too many

people are in it that should not be. They're following the other people that don't know what they don't know and are saving in a place when they have no idea how it works, what it does, what they are paying for it, what it's earning or losing them each year, or where it is going to take them.

If knowing is half the battle, they have lost the battle. They were not even aware they were in a battle! The analogy I used in the prologue of this book about going to war without any training is more accurate than anyone would like to admit.

I have met many people that have fallen into this trap of investing in the wrong direction, and many of them had lost sight of what they were saving for in the first place. When they recognize how much money they lost in the market and how much time it took them to save that money, they lose faith in their plan. They do not think it will get them where they want to go, so they give up on it. Some just stop contributing, but many abandon ship altogether. This isn't because they cannot accomplish their goal; it's because they did not have a plan that they understood and were comfortable with—a plan that they thought had the chance of giving them the retirement that they wanted and dreamed about.

Now as I said, there is a time and place for the market—if you know enough to understand the risk; if you are young enough to be able to overcome any losses in the market due to time being on your side; if you have short-term savings and an account offering you some sort of guarantees that you will not be one of the 93 percent. If at that point you want to take some money and try to hit a home run or want to try some investments that have the ability to yield you a higher return and you know enough to be comfortable with what you are doing with your money, then the market can work for you. But investing in this way provides you with the knowledge that no matter what, even if you lost everything that you had in the market, you would not end up failing to reach your goal for retirement. If, after your retirement goals are met, you still have additional money to invest, the market may be a place for you to do just that.

Now, this may seem like a lot of conditions on when you should invest in the market. When I explain the third method to earning interest, you will better understand why it is that the market should be your last avenue for investing. There simply are better options that have a much higher probability of helping you hit your goals without all the risk that you would need to take in the market.

Before I get there, I do want to address one other item in relation to the market. This is what I call the *golden decade.* I use this term to correlate to the ten-year period before you are going to retire. The reason I refer to it as the golden decade is because during this period of time, you cannot afford to lose anything from your retirement funds. The simple reason for this is that you do not have the time to earn it back if you lose it. Your income-earning years are falling away, and you do not have the time to replace any losses in the market. As I explained earlier, some investors had to wait four to five *years* to earn back their losses from 2008. If you are planning on retiring in the next ten years and you are going to need that money to do it, then you need that money to grow. You cannot afford to lose anything in the ten years prior to, let alone while you are in, retirement. For this reason, you need to make sure that 100 percent of the investment that you will need for your retirement income is in a secure place that still gives you the ability to earn a decent rate of return *and* guarantees you against loss.

Very soon, I will show you how the Armored Personal Retirement Vehicle can protect you from losses in the market and still give you the ability to earn double-digit returns when the market is doing well.

CHAPTER 4

DISTRIBUTION

That's right, distribution. This may be one of the biggest landmines your retirement will ever have to deal with. Many people do not realize this, but proper distribution planning is essential to any retirement plan. Without having a distribution plan in place, how do you know how much you can take out? How do you know how to make your money last so that you don't run out?

THE SNOWBALL EFFECT

As a child, I knew that the easiest way to make a snowman was to start with a snowball. You form a nice round shape in your hands, place it on the ground, and begin rolling. You roll the ball around, changing directions to keep the round shape as it begins to get bigger and bigger. Once you have it the size that you want, you're set. Then it's time to make the middle section, and you start again.

Once a few friends of mine and I decided that we wanted to make a huge snowman. It was a snow day off from school, what else were we going to do? So we started making our snowballs. Now, when these Snowballs get big, they start to get heavy and hard to move around. We realized that it would be a lot easier if we started at the top of a hill. That way we could get the large ball at the bottom of the snowman without too much effort. Luckily—or so I thought— we lived in a cul-de-sac with my house at the very end, and there was a hill up at the top of the street. So I figured that if I went to the top of the hill and started the snowball rolling down the hill, I could get it into the road and roll it right into my front yard. The plan was flawless, at least in the mind of a ten-year-old boy.

So we went to the top of the hill, and I made the starter snowball. It was perfect—I made sure it was round on every side, the perfect shape. I packed it well and I set it down on the top of the hill. Now all it needed was a little nudge to get started. I gave it the nudge, and for the first couple of feet I was careful to make sure that I was turning it to maintain the perfect shape that we wanted for the base of our snowman. And then the snowball began rolling on its own. This was exactly what I had hoped for—I thought it was great! Then the snowball began to gain momentum, and it very quickly became too difficult for me and my friends to control. It rolled down directly towards the Jacksons' house, the first house on our street and the house directly at the end of the hill. It was now almost three feet tall and clearly beyond our ability to stop.

The collision between the snowball and the Jackson home was not as bad as the images that were running through my head at the time. It ended up being a large boom, and the nicely formed snowball was reduced to a mound of snow at the base of their home.

I tell this story for a reason. As we begin taking money out of our retirement accounts, we need to take only what we earn. Otherwise, we may begin to slowly nudge that snowball down a slope that we won't be able to slow its decent, stop, or recover from.

For example, let's say that you have a million dollars in a retirement account and you want to start taking out money for retirement. Let's suppose you've planned well, have no debt, and feel that you can live comfortably on $50,000 per year in retirement. You decide that you want to make sure your money is completely safe, so you put your money in a fixed or money market account earning 1 percent interest. But as soon as you make your first withdrawal, you have unknowingly given that snowball its first nudge. Here's why: in the first year, you take out $50,000 (5 percent of the balance of the account) and earn $9,500, so your account value is reduced to $959,500. The next year, to keep your income the same, you have to take out 5.21 percent of your account's balance to get the same $50,000, but you earn only $9,059 in interest that year. By the third year you are taking out 5.44 percent, and by the tenth year you are taking out 8.68 percent of your retirement account's value just to keep having the same $50,000 each year that you need for retirement income. The snowball is rolling. And with how fast it's going downhill at this point, it would be very tough to stop the quick decline of your account value. And if you don't, you'll end up running out of money in just over 21 years.

Chart 5-A. – Distribution and the Snowball Effect

Year	Balance	Withdrawals	ROR	Interest Earned	Total
0	$1,000,000	$ (50,000)	1.0%	$ 9,500	$ 959,500
1	$ 959,500	$ (50,000)	1.0%	$ 9,095	$ 918,595
2	$ 918,595	$ (50,000)	1.0%	$ 8,685	$ 877,280
3	$ 877,280	$ (50,000)	1.0%	$ 8,272	$ 835,553
4	$ 835,553	$ (50,000)	1.0%	$ 7,855	$ 793,409
5	$ 793,409	$ (50,000)	1.0%	$ 7,434	$ 750,843
6	$ 750,843	$ (50,000)	1.0%	$ 7,008	$ 707,851
7	$ 707,851	$ (50,000)	1.0%	$ 6,578	$ 664,430
8	$ 664,430	$ (50,000)	1.0%	$ 6,144	$ 620,574
9	$ 620,574	$ (50,000)	1.0%	$ 5,705	$ 576,280
10	$ 576,280	$ (50,000)	1.0%	$ 5,262	$ 531,543
11	$ 531,543	$ (50,000)	1.0%	$ 4,815	$ 486,358
12	$ 486,358	$ (50,000)	1.0%	$ 4,363	$ 440,722
13	$ 440,722	$ (50,000)	1.0%	$ 3,907	$ 394,629
14	$ 394,629	$ (50,000)	1.0%	$ 3,446	$ 348,075
15	$ 348,075	$ (50,000)	1.0%	$ 2,980	$ 301,056
16	$ 301,056	$ (50,000)	1.0%	$ 2,510	$ 253,567
17	$ 253,567	$ (50,000)	1.0%	$ 2,035	$ 205,602
18	$ 205,602	$ (50,000)	1.0%	$ 1,556	$ 157,158
19	$ 157,158	$ (50,000)	1.0%	$ 1,071	$ 108,230
20	$ 108,230	$ (50,000)	1.0%	$ 582	$ 58,812
21	$ 58,812	$ (50,000)	1.0%	$ 88	$ 8,900
22	$ 8,900	$ (8,900)	1.0%	$ 0	$ 0

Earlier, I explained the million-dollar misconception and showed how you should take out just the interest that you earn every year. That's really just a simple way to make sure that you don't dip into the principal of your savings and start the snowball rolling. Many clients that I meet with tell me that they don't mind dipping into the principal because they don't have anybody that they need to leave money to when the die. I agree—if you don't have dependents, why do you need to have money left over when you pass away? The problem is that you don't know when you are going to die. This is one of those unknowns that we have to protect ourselves from. If we take more than we're earning, we start the snowball rolling, and there's no way to stop it.

Let's see what happens when we plan for a little more aggressive interest rate at retirement and invest in a safe 5 percent growth account. We know that if you draw only what you earn, you will have income for life, but let's assume that you want to have more income at retirement and be able to enjoy your retirement with additional spending money.

Chart 5-B.

Year	Balance	Withdrawals	ROR	Interest Earned	Total	% of Withdrawal
1	$1,000,000	($90,000)	5.0%	$54,500	$964,500	9%
2	$964,500	($90,000)	5.0%	$52,725	$927,225	9%
3	$927,225	($90,000)	5.0%	$50,861	$888,086	10%
4	$888,086	($90,000)	5.0%	$48,904	$846,990	10%
5	$846,990	($90,000)	5.0%	$46,849	$803,840	11%
6	$803,840	($90,000)	5.0%	$44,692	$758,532	11%
7	$758,532	($90,000)	5.0%	$42,426	$710,958	12%
8	$710,958	($90,000)	5.0%	$40,047	$661,006	13%
9	$661,006	($90,000)	5.0%	$37,550	$608,556	14%
10	$608,556	($90,000)	5.0%	$34,927	$553,484	15%
11	$553,484	($90,000)	5.0%	$32,174	$495,659	16%
12	$495,659	($90,000)	5.0%	$29,282	$434,942	18%
13	$434,942	($90,000)	5.0%	$26,247	$371,189	21%
14	$371,189	($90,000)	5.0%	$23,059	$304,248	24%
15	$304,248	($90,000)	5.0%	$19,712	$233,960	30%
16	$233,960	($90,000)	5.0%	$16,198	$160,159	38%
17	$160,159	($90,000)	5.0%	$12,507	$82,666	56%
18	$82,666	($82,666)	0.0%	$0.00	$0.00	100

Your million dollars is gone in just 18 years even with a comfortable 5 percent return, but what I want you to notice is the last column.

This column shows what percentage of your account you are taking out when you withdraw your income. In the first year, it starts with a simple 9 percent.

Here, we are at the top of the hill, and it's not very steep. In the third year, you withdraw 10 percent, and the fifth year 11 percent. Not too bad, right? But now the hill is starting to get steeper. In years six through twelve, the rate of withdrawal goes from 12 percent to 18 percent. Now the snowball is rolling beyond your ability to control it. In years thirteen through sixteen, you go from 21 percent to 38 percent—*in just three years*! Your investment is about to end up as a small lump of snow at the bottom of the hill.

But if we know how the snowball works, why do most advisors and retirement calculators calculate a retirement based on a set time period? They *plan* on you drawing income for a period of 20 or 25 years. In other words, they *plan* on rolling the snowball down the hill, even when you have *no idea* when you are going to die!

Arriving at retirement is not the end goal here—the goal is *living* through retirement with the finances that you need to provide you the quality of life that you desire! Remember, there is something worse than waking up dead; it's waking up *dead broke*.

Place yourself in this position: you saved for 30 years and were able to save a million dollars. At age 65, you retire, and you decide that you are going to take out $90,000 per year because you don't need to leave a large sum of money to your estate. In this scenario, you are out of money at the age of 82. But what if you live to the age of 92? Those last ten years are not going to be your golden years. You will most likely have lowered your withdrawal amount or started working part time to slow the decent of the snowball. But this is a cycle that is nearly impossible to correct.

Here's the problem: How can I plan on and budget for my retirement when I don't know what my return will be in retirement? Currently, fixed crediting rates are around 3 percent, and since that return varies, how can I really plan my distributions when this year it could be 4 percent and the next it could be 3 percent?

Some people believe that to solve this issue, all we need to do is use methods to earn interest that will give you a better rate of return. The problem with this strategy is that with a higher rate of return comes greater risk. If we have even one year of loss, that loss is compounded by the fact that we are taking money out at the same time. As a result, we start that snowball rolling a lot faster, and it becomes much more difficult to stop and recover from.

Let's assume, under the same scenario, that you lost 10 percent of your account value the first year to the market. If you still took out 5 percent for income, so your account actually lost 15 percent of its value. Next year when you go to take out your $50,000 for income, you have to take out 6 percent of your account value—and that's assuming you break even in the market that year. The snowball has begun to roll. And while you can recover by having strong returns later on, after a 21 percent loss in two years, you would need a 26.5 percent return by the end of that second year just to get back to where you started from. If you had two bad years in a row, the snowball can quickly get out of control.

Understand this simple principle: anytime you draw on your principal, you begin to make your snowball. The question is, how steep is your hill?

In just a couple short chapters, I will show you how

the Armored Personal Retirement Vehicle is designed with income for the rest of your life in mind.

CHAPTER 5

FEES

Fees are like landmines to your retirement. A landmine or an Improvised Explosive Device (IED) can be almost invisible to the unknowing or untrained eye; it may appear to be nothing at all, but that "nothing" can cause a great deal of damage. You think it is just a small fee of 1% but fail to recognize what damage that small fee may come to over a period of time.

So let's take a moment and talk about what fees are. First, understand that almost every financial product out there has fees. The financial company is there to provide a service and to make money in the process. Depending on the product, plan, and type of investment, there are several different types of fees that your account may be subject to. The problem is that most Americans are unaware of those fees and, even worse, the impact that those fees can have on their retirement.

In a study conducted by AARP in November of 2007, they found that 83% of Americans surveyed did not know what the fees were in their 401K.[5] Furthermore, they estimated that in a combined working family with both partners contributing to a 401K, the average family could pay as much as $155,000 in fees over the course of their careers. With the US Census Bureau figuring the average household income in America to be just over $50,000, this would mean the 401k is costing the equivalent of three years' salary!

The United States Department of Labor website uses the following example to illustrate the impact that fees can have on your retirement:

"Assume that you are an employee with 35 years until retirement and a current 401(k) account balance of $25,000. If returns on investments in your account over the next 35 years average 7 percent and fees and expenses reduce your average returns by 0.5 percent, your account balance will grow to $227,000 at retirement. Even if there are no further contributions to your account. If fees and expenses are 1.5 percent, however, your account balance will grow to only $163,000. The 1 percent difference in fees and expenses would reduce your account balance at retirement by 28 percent." [6]

Note the last line: "The 1 percent difference in fees and expenses would reduce your account balance at retirement by 28 percent." *Twenty-eight percent?* Now you see why it's so critical to know the fees that are being charged to your retirement account.

So why are most Americans unaware of the fees that they're being charged? There are several reasons. Mutual fund returns in 401(k) plans are normally reported as net returns, meaning that fees for managing your investments are subtracted from your gains or added to your losses before calculating the annual return. Other costs, such as administrative and record-keeping fees, are often divvied up among plan participants but are not explicitly listed on individual statements.

This was very frustrating to David Loeper, the author of *Stop the 401k Rip-off.* In his book, he explained that as a private investor in his 401k, he was completely unaware of the fees and was shocked, when he tried to identify them, by how difficult it can be to find out how much you are paying. He explains that "Under the expense column, my 401(k) statement said I was paying zero. But in reality, I was paying about $1,500 a year on an average balance of about $120,000, even though the bulk of my investments were in very low-cost index funds." So his statement said he was paying nothing while in reality he was paying over 1.2 percent annually. [7]

Another reason people do not know what they are paying is because there are so many different fees— plan administration fees, investment fees, individual service fees, broker service fees, sales charges, management fees, trade fees, and my personal favorite, "other fees."

New laws have been placed in effect to require companies to disclose their fees in the summary plan description. However, most people do not read this disclosure and remain unaware. In fact, a survey conducted by LIMRA found that roughly the same percentage of participants said that they still did not know how much they paid in plan annual fees and expenses, even after the new disclosures went into effect. So what is the average fee charged in a 401k? The *401(k) Averages Book*[8] found that the average total expense for a small plan in 2012 was 1.46

percent, taking into account all administrative and record-keeping fees.

In the following example, let's assume that a 35-year-old begins contributing $1000 per month into his 401(k). He earns 9.46 percent per year but pays 1.46 percent in fees each year.

4-A. Fees

Year	Balance	Fees	Annual Fees	Cumulative Fees
0	$ 13,135	1.46%	$ 192	$ 192
1	$ 27,513	1.46%	$ 402	$ 593
2	$ 43,251	1.46%	$ 631	$ 1,225
3	$ 60,478	1.46%	$ 883	$ 2,108
4	$ 79,334	1.46%	$ 1,158	$ 3,266
5	$ 99,974	1.46%	$ 1,460	$ 4,726
6	$ 122,567	1.46%	$ 1,789	$ 6,515
7	$ 147,297	1.46%	$ 2,151	$ 8,666
8	$ 174,367	1.46%	$ 2,546	$ 11,212
9	$ 203,997	1.46%	$ 2,978	$ 14,190
10	$ 236,430	1.46%	$ 3,452	$ 17,642
11	$ 271,932	1.46%	$ 3,970	$ 21,612
12	$ 310,792	1.46%	$ 4,538	$ 26,150
13	$ 353,328	1.46%	$ 5,159	$ 31,308
14	$ 399,888	1.46%	$ 5,838	$ 37,147
15	$ 450,852	1.46%	$ 6,582	$ 43,729
16	$ 506,638	1.46%	$ 7,397	$ 51,126
17	$ 567,701	1.46%	$ 8,288	$ 59,414
18	$ 634,541	1.46%	$ 9,264	$ 68,679
19	$ 707,704	1.46%	$ 10,332	$ 79,011
20	$ 787,788	1.46%	$ 11,502	$ 90,513
21	$ 875,448	1.46%	$ 12,782	$ 103,294
22	$ 971,400	1.46%	$ 14,182	$ 117,477
23	$ 1,076,430	1.46%	$ 15,716	$ 133,193
24	$ 1,191,395	1.46%	$ 17,394	$ 150,587
25	$ 1,317,236	1.46%	$ 19,232	$ 169,819
26	$ 1,454,982	1.46%	$ 21,243	$ 191,061
27	$ 1,605,759	1.46%	$ 23,444	$ 214,505
28	$ 1,770,799	1.46%	$ 25,854	$ 240,359
29	$ 1,951,451	1.46%	$ 28,491	$ 268,850
30	$ 2,149,194	1.46%	$ 31,378	$ 300,229

As you can see in this example, with the average 401K fees on his account, this person will pay $300,229 in fees before retirement. And in the last five years before retirement, right when he'll need the money the most, he'll be paying over $20,000 per year. Now, if your account is growing, these fees may not seem outrageous, but let's be clear on this: if you are having a losing year, the fees will compound that loss. That's right, in the example above we were paying fees, but our money was growing. When you are losing, you will pay those fees also, compounding the loss. If you lost 8 percent, you actually lost 9.46 percent with the loss and the fees.

In addition, if you leave your money in the fee-based account during your retirement, your 5 percent distribution withdrawal just went to 6.46 percent. Remember the snowball? Your hill just got a lot steeper.

So can the Armored Personal Retirement Vehicle really provide you with all the protection I've promised and still save you money in fees? Yes! I will outline how much you can save in just one more chapter.

CHAPTER 6

TAXES

Taxes may very well be the largest threat that there is to being able to have income for life. They're also one of the hardest things to work around when planning your retirement income. And why is that, you may ask? It is because we have no way of knowing what your tax rate will be at retirement! Most of the other threats that we have discussed are fairly well known. When you are aware of a threat, it gives you the ability to plan and prepare for it. But an unseen threat can cause a tremendous amount of damage.

Let's look at what our retirement formula looks like so far. During the accumulation phase (before retirement), you can look at how your money is growing and understand the impact if we illustrate it with the following formula:

Money x (Rate of Return – Inflation – Fees) x Time = Wealth

So if you are saving $10,000 per year, you can understand the impact on your account like this: $10,000 x (7% – 2.56% –1.46%) x 30 = $894,000.

This formula will not provide you with an accurate account balance, but it does very simply illustrate the damages that your retirement experienced due to inflation and fees. In this example, we did not even take into account any potential losses in the market—and you can image how that would compound this even further.

Now let's look at the dangers of the distribution phase of your retirement. I will illustrate these dangers using the following formula series:

Account Value x (Rate of Return – Inflation – Fees – Distribution Percentage) = Gross Income

Gross Income – Taxes = Net Income

Net income is the amount of money that you get to put in your pocket each year.

In the distribution phase of our retirement, we have

the same dangers as before, but now we've added two additional threats to the list. This is the *ultimate threat matrix* to your retirement.

The good news is that we're aware of most of these threats. We know the dangers that they pose, and we can plan accordingly, allowing us to reach our goal. Only one factor here threatens the success of the mission, and it does so because it's very difficult to prepare for—we have no way of knowing how much damage it will cause. That threat is how much you will be taxed at retirement.

This is where the investment industry is really missing the point. Let me tell you what these firms teach their employees—and I know this firsthand because I was being taught this very thing. Early in my career, I worked as an employee for a corporation that was my broker dealer. They had all their employees go through training on how to sell and discuss products with clients. The problem was that they were teaching us what they wanted us to say, not what our clients needed to know.

In a training class on qualified accounts, I asked the instructor why we would want a client to put all their money in the 403(b) or IRA that we were selling, only to have them be hit with taxes in their retirement. His answer was short and simple: "Don't worry about that because they'll be in a smaller tax bracket when they retire."

In a way, he was right, but only because the products and plans the company was selling its clients would never have allowed them to reach financial independence! They would have not had the choice but to be in a smaller tax bracket because they never would have been able to get where they needed to go.

The truth is that it depends on what you want your retirement to be. If your house is paid for and you just want enough retirement income to get by, you might be in a smaller tax bracket. But wouldn't you prefer to have your money in a place that gives you the opportunity to keep the same quality of life that you had while you were working? Except instead of worrying about the kids and the mortgage and work, you get to spend that money on *you*—on your hobbies, your interests, and on enjoying time that is now truly yours.

The fact of the matter is that even if you retire in a smaller bracket because your income is lower than it was, it does not mean that you won't be taxed at the same rate. If the tax rate goes up on all the tax brackets, you can still be exposed to a greater tax threat on your retirement. So saying "Don't worry about it" just doesn't cut it for me, not when I'm trying to help my client get where they want to go. Not identifying this threat and assessing the risk that it poses to achieving your goal places the entire mission at risk, so we need to worry about it!

The problem here is that tax rates change. How can I advise my clients on how to prepare for taxes when the rate can change at any time and when those changes can severely impact the outcome?

Let's look at this scenario a little closer so that we can really see it for what it is. Let's say that you did everything right—you saved a lot of money over the years, protected it from loss, watched it grow and were able to shore up a nice nest egg for your retirement. You didn't have any huge plans, except to be able to enjoy a few rounds of golf each month, and maybe travel once or twice a year. But you figure it all out, and by your calculations, you have just enough money to get you through it. You set out knowing exactly how much money you need to budget in order to live the life that you and your wife planned for at retirement. So you retire. Five years later, you're seventy years old, and the tax rate changes from 18 percent to 22 percent. You just lost 4 percent of your fixed income. If you take any more out each year to pay for the increase, you'll start to run out of money. So now you're faced with two options: First, you can cut the golfing and the travel out and just stay close to home and try to get by through better budgeting. But remember inflation keeps eating away at your savings too. Your second option is to find part-time work to make a little extra money so that you can pay the taxes that went up on your retirement savings.

That's right, you did everything you were supposed to—you saved your entire life, invested wisely, planned your income, and figured it all out. Then, due to no fault of your own, a tax law changes, changing your life forever. That is the position that retirees find themselves in when all their retirement money is held in tax-deferred accounts.

I'll take a minute here to discuss the options that you

have for how your money will be taxed while you are saving and when you retire. Understand that I love my country—I will pay what I have to pay. However, the way I look at it is this: They wrote the rules the way they wanted to. So I will abide by those rules and pay the taxes that I have to pay, but I will not pay a penny more than I have to.

You have two options for how your money will be taxed. The first option is to be taxed annually. So if we have an investment worth $10,000 and it earned 10 percent that year, then you earned $1000, right? But then, at the end of the year, your bank sent you a 1099-INT, and the IRS comes and takes their part, and then the state comes and takes their part, before you know it your 10 percent return can be closer to a 6.5 percent return. Now, earlier I explained how even one percentage point can potentially mean tens of thousands of dollars to you over time. So it does not make sense to pay the taxes on the money every year. This is exactly why most people save for retirement in accounts designed to avoid annual taxes.

These accounts are known as tax-deferred accounts. There are several types, like the IRA (408), 401(k), and 403(b) (all of these numbers refer to the Internal Revenue Code, or IRC, that governs the account). That code dictates how you can put money in the account and how you can take it out. Now, who is really calling the shots on these accounts? The IRS. That's right, it is really theirs to control. You can put money in and take money out, but only in accordance with the IRS code that they wrote to control that account. And if you do anything different than they permit, you will pay hefty penalties and huge fees.

Let's talk about the benefits of these accounts so that you can see why people are willing to allow the IRS to dictate to them what they can and can't do with their own money.

First off, you don't have to pay the taxes on the interest every year. So as long as the money remains in your account, it continues to grow. The interest you earn compounds naturally because it's not being taken out to pay taxes every year.

The other big upside is free money. If you work for an employer that is willing to match employee contributions dollar for dollar into their company

401(k), you basically double your money for free. This is a huge benefit. You should look closely to see if the company plan can play a role in your retirement so that you can grab this free money.

Now let's discuss the downsides of tax-deferred accounts. First off, what would you rather be taxed on—a small amount of money, or a large amount of money? Often when I ask my clients this, they think it's a trick question. Who would rather be taxed on a large amount of money? But that is exactly what most Americans are doing. They save in an IRA or a 401(k) and they take the tax benefits now on the small amount of money that they put into their account. What they do not realize is that in so doing they have agreed that the IRS will share the interest that they earn on their money, starting the day that they begin to take the money out. I would gladly pay the taxes on the $100 that I save now if they promise to leave alone the $10,000 that I take later! But that's not how tax-deferred accounts work. When you retire on a tax-deferred account, you agree to pay taxes on the money that you live on in retirement.

So being taxed on the growth is the first downside to these accounts. The next downside I will pose in the form of a question: What rate are you going to be taxed at in retirement? Do you think that taxes are going to go down or up in the next 20 years before your retirement, or even throughout the 20 years of your retirement? That's right, there is no way of knowing what that rate will be. However, with the national debt being where it is, and our tax rate currently being lower than the historical average, it is not hard to envision the tax rate being higher down the road than it is today.

This is even more of a threat when your home is paid off and you have lost that tax deduction. Your kids, your work expenses, and all these other things that you used to have to lower your tax liabilities are now gone, and you are completely exposed to whatever damage the IRS chooses to inflict upon your retirement.

The third downside are some of the limitations that the IRS poses on these types of accounts. The 59.5 rule, or early distribution penalty, that states that you cannot take money out of your qualified account except in very specific circumstances. If you do decide to take money out of your account before you reach the age of 59.5 years old, you will pay regular income taxes on that money in addition to a 10 percent penalty.

Some tax-deferred accounts have annual contribution limitations, which may restrict you from saving as much as you need in order to have the income you want at retirement. The higher your income, the less effective these accounts become due to the contribution limitations. And then there is the 70.5 rule. This one says that for whatever reason, if you do not start taking money out of your accounts prior to the year that you attain the age of 70.5, you must begin to take out what the IRS says that you have to take out. If you do not, they will levy a 50 percent excise tax on the amount that they say that you should have taken out of your account.

With all these rules and limitations, you can see why I look at these accounts as "theirs." They are the ones calling the shots on your account.

The last option is to place your money in accounts that have tax advantages to them, such as municipal bonds & Roth IRA, which allow you to invest an already taxed dollar and thus not have to pay taxes on the money when you take it out. Now, understand that you *do pay taxes* on the money that goes into the account, so these are not tax free; however, you do not have to pay taxes on the money when you take it out—including on the interest that you earned, which means that you never pay any taxes on the interest from a Roth IRA.

The Armored Personal Retirement Vehicle is another account that gives you tax-advantaged benefits, allowing you to draw income for life that you do not have to pay taxes on—entirely eliminating the tax factor from the threat matrix.

CHAPTER 7

THE ARMORED

PERSONAL

RETIREMENT VEHICLE

By now you should have an understanding of several of the problems that we face in trying to reach our retirement goals. In fact, with so many issues working against us, it's no wonder that only 7 percent of Americans can retire at the age of 65. Most are not aware of the dangers that they need to overcome, and even fewer know how to keep these hazards from preventing them from reaching their primary target. We have to first identify the threats, and second, plan for how to safeguard our retirement from those threats.

Enter the Armored Personal Retirement Vehicle. Our armed forces use Armored Personnel Vehicles to move our troops from place to place in hazardous situations. If you know you have a high probability of taking enemy fire during a trip, it wouldn't make sense to take the family minivan! As I have already explained, your retirement will be exposed to threats much like enemy fire every day.

Much the same way, there is one class of investment that can help move your retirement from where you are now to your retirement goal. Keeping our eyes on the target, we remember that the primary goal is a retirement income that provides you with the money that you need in a retirement that you cannot outlive. That is the goal, the objective, the primary target. No matter what analogy we use here, it is essential that we keep our eye on the target: *income for life*. And whatever plan puts the most money in your pocket for the rest of your life without running out should be the vehicle that you use to get there.

Enter indexed insurance products. Indexed universal life insurance policies and fixed indexed annuities can help you avoid or minimize the damages your retirement account can experience, allowing you to reach your goal without losing hundreds of thousands of dollars to some of the hazards that we've discussed in this book—and some we haven't gone over yet.

Let's start by explaining how indexed insurance products can protect you from these hazards.

INFLATION

Inflation is a hazard that we will need to protect ourselves from throughout our entire lives—not just while our money is growing but also while we are taking distributions and enjoying our retirement. Inflation never sleeps. It may change, slow, or accelerate, but it will always be there, and we must always protect ourselves from it.

Let's assume that you had a retirement income goal of $80,000 per year. You are ecstatic when you realize you have enough saved to be able to begin living the life that you've dreamed of and planned for. However, let's recall the rule of 72. While this rule works for how your money grows, it also works the other way. This means that we can use the same rule to determine how the cost of living will grow and how this will affect your amazing retirement. If the

Consumer Price Index averages a 3 percent rate of growth, we can figure that every 24 years, the cost of living will double. That's right, double! So even though we arrived at our retirement objective, we're still under fire and still require protection from inflation.

In this example of retiring at 65 with $80,000 per year, 12 short years later you are 77, and now the purchasing power of your retirement income has lowered to just $60,000. By the age of 89, it is down to just *half* of your income goal. And while you may not be as active at 89 as you were at 65, our expenses have probably changed by then too. You may have more medical expenses and possibly several more grandchildren to spoil, so the reduction in your income as a result of inflation will slowly degrade your retirement.

Several Insurance products have riders, or features, available that will allow you to protect your income from inflation.

These products allow you to begin taking money out of your account at the level that you intended, and then your income increases every year for a set period based on the annual Consumer Price Index increase. This allows your income to grow every year in direct correlation to the increase in your expenses over the course of your retirement. This feature can work differently based on the company or product, but it typically means that you take a little less money out initially. However, you are then typically getting more out each and every year thereafter. Within a short time frame you are getting more money every year than you would have gotten without the inflation protection.

Below, I have a table that shows how your income would increase by using an inflation protection rider. Let's assume that you began taking income out of your account at the age of 65. If you had non-increasing income, your income would start at $95,055 per year and would remain the same until you passed away at age 90. You would have taken a total of $2,471,430 in retirement income over the course of your 25-year retirement.

Now, if you opted for inflation protection, you would start with a lower income of $80,643 in the first year, but within seven years, you are taking more income per year than you would have without the protection.

Your income will then continue to increase by 3 percent each year. By the age 75, you are taking $105,261.88 in income each year, and by 85 you will have $137,396.46 in annual income. By the time you passed away, at the age of 90 you will have taken a total of $2,944,907 in income. An increase of $473,477 from the level income.

Chart 7-A. Inflation protected income.

Age	Withdrawal	Total Withdraws	Withdrawal	Total Withdraws
65	$ 95,055.00	$ 95,055.00	$ 80,643.00	$ 80,643.00
66	$ 95,055.00	$ 190,110.00	$ 82,820.36	$ 163,463.36
67	$ 95,055.00	$ 285,165.00	$ 85,056.51	$ 248,519.87
68	$ 95,055.00	$ 380,220.00	$ 87,353.04	$ 335,872.91
69	$ 95,055.00	$ 475,275.00	$ 89,711.57	$ 425,584.48
70	$ 95,055.00	$ 570,330.00	$ 92,133.78	$ 517,718.26
71	$ 95,055.00	$ 665,385.00	$ 94,621.39	$ 612,339.65
72	$ 95,055.00	$ 760,440.00	$ 97,176.17	$ 709,515.82
73	$ 95,055.00	$ 855,495.00	$ 99,799.93	$ 809,315.75
74	$ 95,055.00	$ 950,550.00	$ 102,494.53	$ 911,810.27
75	$ 95,055.00	$ 1,045,605.00	$ 105,261.88	$ 1,017,072.15
76	$ 95,055.00	$ 1,140,660.00	$ 108,103.95	$ 1,125,176.10
77	$ 95,055.00	$ 1,235,715.00	$ 111,022.75	$ 1,236,198.85
78	$ 95,055.00	$ 1,330,770.00	$ 114,020.37	$ 1,350,219.22
79	$ 95,055.00	$ 1,425,825.00	$ 117,098.92	$ 1,467,318.14
80	$ 95,055.00	$ 1,520,880.00	$ 120,260.59	$ 1,587,578.73
81	$ 95,055.00	$ 1,615,935.00	$ 123,507.63	$ 1,711,086.36
82	$ 95,055.00	$ 1,710,990.00	$ 126,842.33	$ 1,837,928.69
83	$ 95,055.00	$ 1,806,045.00	$ 130,267.07	$ 1,968,195.76
84	$ 95,055.00	$ 1,901,100.00	$ 133,784.29	$ 2,101,980.05
85	$ 95,055.00	$ 1,996,155.00	$ 137,396.46	$ 2,239,376.51
86	$ 95,055.00	$ 2,091,210.00	$ 141,106.17	$ 2,380,482.68
87	$ 95,055.00	$ 2,186,265.00	$ 141,106.17	$ 2,521,588.85
88	$ 95,055.00	$ 2,281,320.00	$ 141,106.17	$ 2,662,695.02
89	$ 95,055.00	$ 2,376,375.00	$ 141,106.17	$ 2,803,801.19
90	$ 95,055.00	$ 2,471,430.00	$ 141,106.17	$ 2,944,907.36

The best part of this is that when you begin drawing income, you get to determine which one you want. *You do not have to decide today.* So when you get to your retirement, you will have the option of the higher upfront income or the income that increases over time.

INVESTMENT LOSS / RISK

The third way to grow your money is known as indexed growth. This type of interest crediting is done only inside insurance products, whether it be in an Indexed Universal Life (IUL) insurance policy or a Fixed Indexed Annuity (FIA). Let me explain exactly how it works so that you can see how powerful this can be in helping you see a great rate of return without any potential for loss. That's right, in these products you will be 100 percent guaranteed not to lose money due to a market downturn. They even offer a minimum guaranteed rate of return.

Here's how it works. When the market goes up, you get to see the upside of the market, limited by what is known as a cap. (Some indexed products limit using participation rates or spreads, but for simplicity, I will focus on caps.) In exchange for that cap, when the market goes down, you have the guarantee that you will not lose anything—not the principal that you put into your account or the interest that you've earned. So in exchange for capping your growth, say, at 12 percent, these programs offer you a minimum guaranteed rate of return. You can look at the cap as your ceiling and the minimum rate as your floor. You earn whatever interest the market provides you between your ceiling and your floor. So if your cap was 12 percent and the market earned 7 percent, you would earn 7 percent. If the market did 14 percent, you would only earn 12 percent. But here's the best part—if the market lost 8 percent the next year, you wouldn't lose a penny. You'd stay right where you were. If the market recovers in the next year, you start from where you left off instead of starting 8 percent lower.

Often, clients ask me how this is possible. Sometimes they think that the insurance company is risking their money to do this. Understand this: if their money was at risk, then yours would be too. Specifically, you would be risking that they would still be in business and able to honor their contract with you when you were ready to retire. If they are taking losses so that you don't, they couldn't stay in business.

Let me use an analogy to show you how this works. Let's say that I was selling a home and you were interested in buying it. You decided that you wanted to get to know the neighbors, the school, and what the commute would be like before you committed to purchasing the home. So you ask me if I would be willing to do a lease option on the home. The lease option says that you will lease my home from me for the next year, and at the end of that year you agree to pay the full asking price of $500,000 for the home. However, you reserve the option to not complete the purchase at the end of that year. You have the ability to walk away; I do not. So we enter into the contract. Now, let's assume that a year later, the value of the house has increased to $700,000 due to changes in the housing market. You have the ability, and a contract, that says that I must sell you the house for $500,000 even though the value of the house is now $700,000. Do you buy it? Absolutely! You just made $200,000 on the purchase of your home. You have immediate equity in it.

Now, let's assume that the housing market went the other way, and after your one-year lease was over, the house was worth only $300,000. Well, you now have the option to either buy the house at the $500,000 price or walk away. This decision is about as easy as the last one. Even if you loved the house, you would not want to pay me $500,000 for a home that was only worth $300,000. You'd most likely walk away from the house, and the only thing that you lost was the lease payments that you had made for that year.

This is essentially how the indexed strategy works in insurance products. The insurance company invests the money that you put in your account in very safe, low-yield investments. They then take the interest that they earned and use the majority of it to purchase options on a stock index like the S&P 500. They purchase the ability to buy the index at today's rates one year from today. The options that they purchase dictate the cap, spread, and participation rate. The insurance company is spending millions to purchase these options, so they're able to offer you a higher cap based on the amount that they are paying. If the market goes up, they buy in; if the index falls, they walk away. Using this method, neither you nor the financial company that you are working with has any money at risk.

This very powerful tool can allow you to see potentially double-digit growth in the good years and no potential for loss if the market goes down. In 2014, most of my clients who have these products saw an average 20 percent or higher increase. Plus, they're protected so that if the market goes down next year, they won't lose a penny.

When meeting with clients, I have found that most people are looking for a way to invest that makes sense. When the market is doing well, we want to earn a decent rate of return. But when the market goes down, we don't want to personally pay for it.

This is exactly what indexing allows you to do. Indexing is like an autopilot feature for your retirement—you don't have to make changes to your account when the market is changing. It's an investment method that lets you beat the inflation battle and see growth without any concern for loss.

FEES

We already know the threat that fees can pose to

your retirement. How does an insurance product protect you from fees? As I previously mentioned, *all* products have some fees—the key here is to minimize the risk and damage that those fees can cause to your retirement. I want to be clear on one thing: there are charges within a life insurance policy; that includes the cost of the insurance. But then, you're actually *purchasing* life insurance, which protects your family if you should pass away, so I don't believe that's a fee. It's a cost for a service that you would typically be buying anyway. However, to give you a side-by-side comparison, we need to look at any cost that reduces your account value or growth as a fee. So for the purpose of argument, we will treat the cost of insurance as a "fee" in this chapter.

Compare the fees that you might pay in a 401(k) or managed brokerage account to the fees, costs, and expenses that you may be paying in an indexed universal life insurance policy. In Chapter 4, I gave the example of a 35-year-old that was saving $1000 per month in his 401(k), and we discussed the total that he would have paid in 401(k) fees based upon an average fee cost of 1.46 percent. Recall that over the course of his 30-year deferment he ended up paying $300,229. In the following chart, I outline all the fees in a typical IUL policy.

Chart 7-B. Policy Fees

Year	Fees	Cost of Insurance	Total Charges	Cumulative Charges
0	$ 3,267	$ 917	$ 4,184	$ 4,184
1	$ 7,450	$ 950	$ 4,216	$ 8,400
2	$ 11,666	$ 998	$ 4,264	$ 12,664
3	$ 15,931	$ 1,059	$ 4,326	$ 16,990
4	$ 20,256	$ 1,111	$ 4,377	$ 21,367
5	$ 24,634	$ 1,096	$ 4,363	$ 25,730
6	$ 28,997	$ 1,086	$ 4,353	$ 30,083
7	$ 33,349	$ 1,082	$ 4,348	$ 34,431
8	$ 37,698	$ 1,055	$ 4,322	$ 38,753
9	$ 42,019	$ 1,011	$ 4,277	$ 43,030
10	$ 43,720	$ 1,070	$ 1,760	$ 44,790
11	$ 45,480	$ 1,127	$ 1,817	$ 46,607
12	$ 47,297	$ 1,183	$ 1,873	$ 48,480
13	$ 49,170	$ 1,255	$ 1,945	$ 50,425
14	$ 51,115	$ 1,318	$ 2,008	$ 52,433
15	$ 53,123	$ 1,387	$ 2,077	$ 54,510
16	$ 55,200	$ 1,448	$ 2,138	$ 56,648
17	$ 57,338	$ 1,496	$ 2,186	$ 58,834
18	$ 59,524	$ 1,539	$ 2,229	$ 61,063
19	$ 61,753	$ 1,565	$ 2,255	$ 63,318
20	$ 64,008	$ 1,583	$ 2,273	$ 65,591
21	$ 66,281	$ 1,590	$ 2,280	$ 67,871
22	$ 68,561	$ 1,584	$ 2,274	$ 70,145
23	$ 70,835	$ 1,549	$ 2,239	$ 72,384
24	$ 73,074	$ 1,468	$ 2,158	$ 74,542
25	$ 75,232	$ 1,328	$ 2,018	$ 76,560
26	$ 690	$ 1,241	$ 2,018	$ 78,578
27	$ 690	$ 1,443	$ 1,931	$ 80,509
28	$ 690	$ 1,659	$ 2,133	$ 82,642
29	$ 690	$ 1,880	$ 2,349	$ 84,991
30	$ 690	$ 1,880	$ 2,570	$ 87,561

Keep in mind that fees and expenses in a policy vary by company, product, and the rating determined by the underwriting of the policy. Expenses listed above are based upon one of the highest-rated IUL products in the world at a standard non-tobacco rating.

Anyone who says that life insurance would cost you too much, does not know what they're talking about! Here are the numbers—against $300,299 in fees in the 401(k), a UIL policy costs just $87,561! That is a savings of $212,738 in fees you didn't have to pay—a savings of 71 percent. Even better, it provided your family with life insurance that you needed to have anyway. If I were to take out the cost of insurance, it would have only cost you $47,155 in actual fees. The cost of insurance, importantly, is what provides you with the tax advantages. Even with this additional cost of the policy, you would have the equivalent of an annual fee of only 0.425 percent. It would be very difficult to find any type of compounding investment that costs less than 0.425 percent once you added up all of your fees and averaged them out.

DISTRIBUTION

We understand the distribution problem and snowball effect, but how does an insurance based retirement account protect us from these potential landmines? Insurance products, including life and annuity products, are designed around an individual's life expectancy. Insurance companies are the experts at determining probable longevity and spreading out income over that anticipated life expectancy. They are so good at it they have products that can guarantee your income for life.

This is done using a life expectancy amortization table. This table is calculated differently for different products and different companies, but they all have the same basic principles. If I have money in an annuity, I have several options available to me: I can take lump sum withdrawals, or I can take income. This income is calculated by the company, and they will give you several options. Some common income options include income for life, income for period certain, and income for survivor. The insurance company will agree to pay this income out for the agreed-upon period of time. If I choose income for life, the insurance company will begin paying me a set amount of money every year till the day I die. This lets me know what my income will be and ensures that I will never run out of money. When making plans on your distribution, your agent will be able to go over your options and help you determine which option best suits your needs.

When I discuss annuities with clients, they often

have misconceptions about them. They typically think that the annuity company gets all the money. This may be due to the fact that historically, when you took income from an annuity, you would annuitize it. The present-day fact is that most annuities now allow you to draw income off of the account without actually annuitizing it. When the annuitant passes away, the balance of the account then gets paid to the beneficiaries listed on the account. A huge benefit of an annuity is that the proceeds avoid probate in the event of death and get paid directly to the beneficiaries. Many annuities also offer an income rider, which will guarantee a specific rate of return as you defer your retirement and then guarantee you income for the rest of your life. Many of these riders also offer features that allow for increases in your income to protect against inflation in retirement. Other features can include the ability to increase your income if you become disabled. Discuss all these options and features with your agent to determine which options are most important to you based on how you plan on using the funds in your account.

Indexed universal life insurance policies have similar features, and those distributions will be discussed in the next section.

TAXES

If you've read this far, you understand how important it is to protect your income from the potential loss and uncertainty that taxes could pose to your retirement. Now let's discuss how indexed universal life insurance products can help you eliminate this ominous threat.

As you may be aware, death benefits paid from life insurance policies are income tax–free in most instances. Now let's talk about how you can use the policy to provide benefits while you're still living.

Cash value life insurance policies give you the ability to access the money in your account in several different ways. You can take a withdrawal from your account, and it is not taxable as long as you are taking out your principal. This is known as your basis, and a withdrawal from your basis is tax free due to the fact that you already paid taxes on the money you put into the policy. Now, if you took out money above your basis, this is your interest—and if you take the interest out as a withdrawal, it will be taxable income in the year that you take it out.

Most policies, however, give you the ability to use the cash value in your policy as collateral for a loan. The insurance company agrees to loan you some of their money while leaving your money in your policy. Since this is classified as a loan instead of a withdrawal, the money that you take out is not taxable. However, to be classified as a loan, there are a few requirements that must be met. The first one is that the loan must be repaid. The insurance company agrees that they will allow you to repay the loan out of the death benefit of the policy when you die. The other requirement is that you must be charged interest, so your insurance company will charge you an interest rate on any of the money that you have borrowed from your policy. This interest rate is typically determined in your contract and can be a fixed rate or a variable rate. Some policies have both as an option, allowing you, the policyholder, to decide how you would like your interest calculated. In most instances, a variable interest rate will follow a bond rate and thereby be competitive with current interest rates.

Now let's look at how this really works.

Let's assume that you have a policy and begin taking loans on your policy each year to live off of for income. The loans are tax–free, so the IRS cannot tax you on that source of income. Your money remains in your account, and the company loans you money from their general funds. The money in your account continues accruing interest at whatever indexed rate that you are currently earning. In this example, we'll assume that the index is currently crediting you interest at a rate of 8 percent. If the loan rate is 4 percent, then you'd be earning 8 percent on all of your money and paying 4 percent on your loan. In effect, you would be earning 4 percent interest, even on money that you have taken out of your account!

Being able to take money out of your account in this way allows you to put more money in your pocket over time than you could using most other typical retirement accounts. This happens for two reasons. The first is the positive arbitrage on your money; which is the ability to earn interest on money that you're living on.

The second reason, is I only have to take out what I

need. If I want to live off of $95,000 per year and I have a tax-free account, I only need to take out the $95,000 that I want. If this was a taxable account, I would need to take out additional funds to cover the taxes on that income. At a 28 percent tax rate, I would have to withdrawal $121,600 each year to have the same amount of money to live on. That's $26,600 extra that you have to take out every year just to pay taxes on your retirement! Taking this additional money out every year reduces your account value very quickly, and it puts zero additional money in your pocket!

CHAPTER 8

ADDITIONAL BENEFITS

OF INSURANCE

PRODUCTS

Life can throw grenades in your direction, and you need to be able to know how your plan will work for you should any of these unforeseen events try to hinder your progress toward your goal. The fact that your plan gives you protection from these potential hazards provides you that extra level of protection that you hope that you will never need.

LAWSUIT AND BANKRUPTCY

Recently, a Property and Casualty Insurance company put out a commercial illustrating the need for people to ensure that they were properly covered. The commercial showed a family in a courtroom being sued because their teenage son was involved in an accident. In the commercial, the judge decreed an award to the plaintiff. The plaintiff's attorney comes over to the defendants' table and says, "Well, the policy only offers coverage up to $250,000. What other assets do they have?" The defendants' attorney states, "Not a lot; there is the savings, and they have a 401(k)." The frightened couple looks at each other, realizing that their retirement accounts are now being threatened and potentially lost based on an accident that they were not properly prepared for. The plaintiffs' attorney asks them to send him a list of the assets, implying that he would be going after them in order to fulfil the court-awarded settlement.

While this commercial was intended to reinforce the need to review your policies and ensure that you are properly covered, it reflects the reality that many retirement accounts can be attacked by court-ordered awards and settlements. Having your savings in an insurance product may offer you an added level of protection against lawsuits and even creditor protection in the event of a bankruptcy.

For example, the state of Arizona does allow you to exempt life insurance policies from being taken by both bankruptcy and creditors—on both the death benefit of your policy and the cash value in your policy. These protections are available to you as long as your dependents are listed as beneficiaries and you have had the policy for two years prior to the claim being made. So you cannot purchase a policy for the purpose of protecting yourself from a lawsuit, but if you had one prior to becoming involved in the lawsuit, you would be protected.

The level of protection varies by state, so you may need to see what your state allows in regard to these exemptions. If you would like information on how these protections would be handled in your state, feel free to contact me on my website at www.aprvbook.com. I can provide you with the information that you need. If you have an agent that you are working with, they can let you know of the protections that are offered in your state.

EMERGENCY NEED

There may be times in our lives when we need to access retirement money in order to overcome an obstacle. Understand that your retirement is a long-term plan. Any time you remove money from a retirement account, it can change whether you hit your income goal within the time that you had hoped. That being said, since these accounts are not subject to the limitations and rules dictated by the IRS, most of these accounts give you the ability to access your cash value even before you turn 59.5 years old. I always recommend that my clients have a short-term account for an emergency fund, and I typically recommend that this short-term account have between three and six months of income in it.

I explained earlier in the book that your contract with the insurance company will allow you to take money out or borrow against your cash value at any time. With the level of access that you have to your account after the first four or five years, your policy can become a very powerful tool that allows you to start putting more money in the policy. This gives you the ability to start transitioning money out of your short-term savings account. Most savings accounts now pay a very low rate of return, and having six months of income in it can leave you losing purchasing power on that money. If you can access your policy cash within ten days, you don't need to have as much money in an account that's not earning any interest for you. I usually start transitioning my clients' short-term funds in the third or fourth year of the policy, and at that point they only need to have 60 days' worth of income in their short-term account.

DEATH

The fact that this is a life insurance policy means that it provides your spouse and dependents with the ultimate protection—replacement of your income at the time they need it most.

In fact, 30 percent of American households do not have any life insurance at all. [9] On top of that, 50 percent of the insured have less than half of what they think they need. These figures show that most Americans need to purchase additional life insurance to protect their families.

Because this retirement vehicle provides you with a death benefit, there's an additional gain available to your family in the event that you should pass away while still working towards your retirement goal.

Your agent will be able to discuss what your insurance need is and make suggestions on how to incorporate your current policy and insurance needs with the plan that they put together for you.

In the next chapter, I will discuss how the policy should be set up in order to ensure the highest income possible in retirement. Make sure that your agent is aware of your insurance needs so that they can help find the balance that will provide you with both benefits.

BANK ON YOURSELF

I've shown how you can take money from your retirement policy by using the loan provisions in the policy. We've also discussed the fact that you have access to your money prior to the age of 59.5 and can use it for emergencies. Now, let's touch on how powerful the fact that you have access to your money prior to retirement can be. I will not go in-depth here because this topic has been covered in detail in other books; I just want to explain the concept.

If you have money in an account that you have

access to, you can use it for any reason. So let's assume that you started saving $1,000 per month at the age of 30. Ten years later, at an interest rate of 8 percent, you have an account value of over $140,000. Now you decide that you would like to purchase a new truck. Rather than getting a loan from the bank or credit union, you can take the money out of your policy in order to purchase the truck. You calculate what your payment would have been on the truck with a reasonable interest rate. Let's assume that you'd pay 8 percent.

The IRS says that you are allowed to pay yourself a "reasonable interest rate," Well, if you are paying 4 percent on your loan from your policy, you could argue that a 4 percent net interest rate would be "reasonable," Let's look at how that works for you. If you were to purchase a new truck for $50,000 and pay for it over six years at an 8 percent interest rate, your payment would be $876.66 per month. You increase your insurance payment from $1000 to $1,876. Like magic, your loan from your policy is repaid *to* your policy. You net a 12.5 percent rate of return on the money that you took out to buy your truck! Indexed growth of 8.5 percent on your account balance + 8 percent that you are paying yourself on the loan – 4 percent loan rate from the insurance company = 12.5 percent interest on money that you used to buy a truck.

If you would like more detailed information on how banking on yourself works, you can talk to your agent. There's a great book written by Nelson Nash titled *Becoming Your Own Banker*. I highly recommend it if you want to understand how to use your policy to finance anything you need. Your business, auto, or even home loan can be financed this way. Remember, this is your money. Make it work for you.

CHILD SAVINGS

I previously explained the critical role time plays in your retirement. In the example in Chapter 2, I showed how a $10,000 investment could grow to $640,000 in 36 years. In that example, we started saving at the age of 29. Now notice how much that $640,000 would have grown to if it had been allowed to grow for another six-year doubling period. The $640,000 would grow to $1,280,000, simply by starting to save at 23 instead of 29. Let's see how far this can go. If we started at 17, it would have been $2,560,000; if we started at 11, it would have been $5,120,000. If we put away for our children at the age of five and they averaged a 12 percent compounding interest rate until the age of 65, they would have $10,240,000 in their account. *Time* is the key element here.

I often meet with clients who are concerned about where they are saving for their children's college fund. Using a plan like this, you can provide your child with all the protections that we have discussed and the ability to take money out for college. I often work with parents on a plan that has them saving for college and then, after the child has gotten employment, they start putting $100–$150 into the plan each month. This single vehicle becomes a permanent life policy, a college fund, a retirement account, and a financial tool giving all the benefits that I have outlined. And it was all done when they were young, giving them the value of time.

CHAPTER 9

MISCONCEPTIONS

ABOUT INSURANCE

There are a few common misconceptions about insurance, and I hope that I have addressed the majority of them already. Things like, "Policies are too expensive," "They have too many fees," "You can't get your money out," and my personal favorite, "Why would you buy insurance for your retirement?" I would like to address two of the other misconceptions out there. They can be cleared up by explaining exactly how the plan works.

BUY TERM AND INVEST THE DIFFERENCE

How your plan is put together makes all the difference in the world. And I have to tell you that there are a lot of people out there selling these products that do not understand how to design a plan to best suit the needs of their clients. I will touch on that in the next chapter. When I'm putting together a plan, if the client tells me that his primary focus is income at retirement, I begin putting together a plan that has the minimum amount of insurance possible while still being considered an insurance product.

I told you how the IRS gets to write the rules. We just need to work within those rules, right? Well, the IRS knows that we are using the tax advantages in life insurance policies to provide tax-free income in retirement, so they've written what is known as the Modified Endowment Contract (MEC) guidelines. These guidelines establish how much money a person can save in an insurance product based on how much insurance they have.

When I design a plan, I want the smallest amount of money possible going to the insurance and as much as possible going to the investment. In order to accomplish this, I routinely design plans for minimum insurance and maximum funding. This is just opposite of how you would ordinarily purchase insurance:

9-A. Typical Insurance Balance

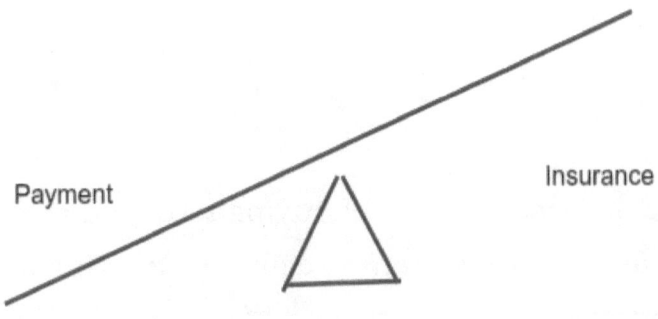

Most people purchase insurance by getting quotes for their policy and then purchase the policy that gives them the insurance they need at the lowest cost. When designing a plan for your retirement, we need to do just the opposite. We need to ask: What is the least amount of insurance that I have to buy in order to put away the money that I want to for retirement?

9-B. Investment Insurance Balance

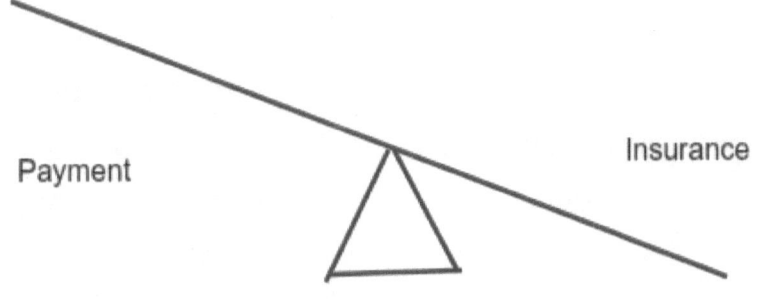

When properly done, the policy should give you

flexibilty in your payments and additional insurance. If you require more insurance to protect your family, that needs to be taken into account. Additional insurance can be added to the policy to satisfy both objectives.

Now to address the idea of buying term and investing the difference. Let's start be defining Term Insurance. You purchase term insurance for a set number of years, typically 20 or 30. The shorter the time, the lower the price. At the end of the term the policy is over so you no longer have insurance. It does provide you with the coverage durring that period and costs less because the risk is lower. When they say buy term invest the difference, they are saying that a permanent insuance product (one that never expires) often costs "too much." So they suggest that instead of saving in one insurance product, you should purchase two different products. One the term insurance policy to protect your family, and the second is the investment product. The idea and concept is fairly simple. If you need $1,000,000 to protect your family, you should purchase a million-dollar term policy for $150 per month, then take the other $350 that you would have paid for a permanent product and put that $350 into an investment account. Then, when your account value increases, you can lower your insurance proportionately. So if your account value reaches $100,000, you can now lower your insurance to $900,000 in insurance, then take the savings and add that to your monthly investment. Slowly, you will be moving more and more money into your investment and purchasing less and less insurance.

Let's look at this for a moment. There are several issues wth this concept.

First off, the foundation of the concept is that permanent insurance is just too expensive. We already discussed this issue when we looked at the fees. And as we discussed the fees inside this type of policy are a fraction of the expenses in a 401(k). To think that purchasing two different products would be cheaper than purchasing just the IUL is not very realistic.

Second, you only need to buy enough insurance to cover your exposure. This statement is actually correct, but let me show you how an IUL does just that.

You have two options when purchasing a permanent policy. Option one is a level-face amount, which means that when your account value grows, your death benefit remains the same.

9-C. Level Death Benefit

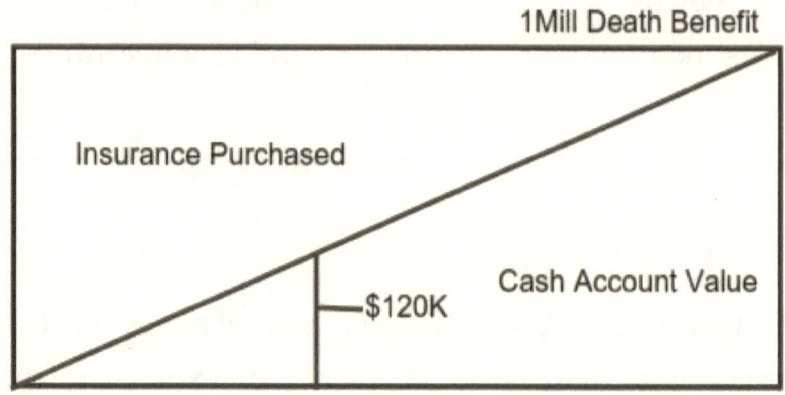

This illustration shows what happens every time you make a payment on such a policy. Your cash value increases, and the amount of insurance that you are buying lowers. The insurance company is only selling you insurance for the amount that they are at risk for. Over time, your insurance decreases and the differenc goes into your cash value.

This means that the level-death benefit policy actually applies to the concept of buying only the insurance that you need investing the rest of the money. Except that here it is on auto-pilot! You don't have to call in and lower your insurance, you don't have to pay for and manage two different products, and you don't have to worry about losing 38 percent of your investment and then having to increase your insurance again ten years later when you may not even be able to qualify for it because of health issues.

Option two is an increasing face amount. This allows the death benefit on your policy to remain static at one million dollars, and when you pass away, your beneficiaries get both the one million in insurance and your cash account value too.

9-D. Increasing Death Benefit

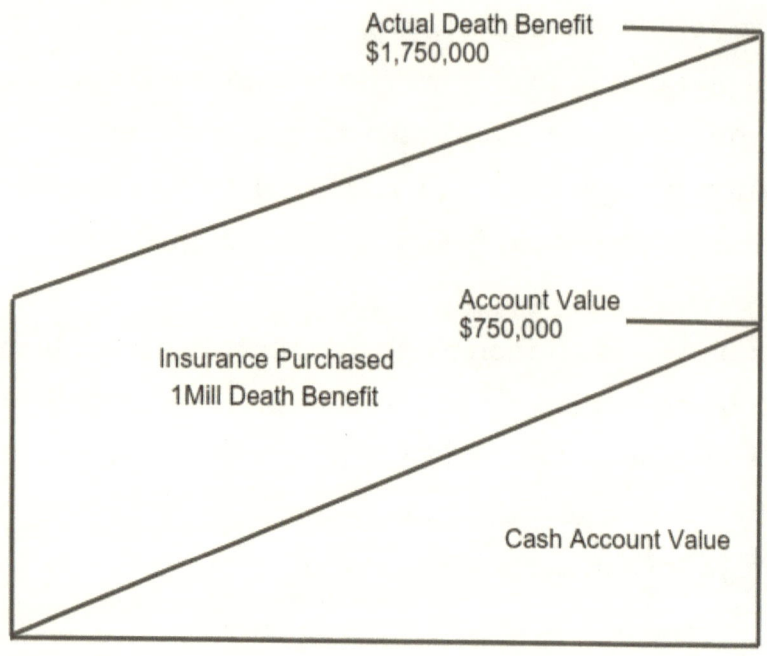

With Option two, your family will get paid both the million-dollar death benefit and the money in your account value if you pass away.

There are many reasons why you may want option two in your plan. But here is why you do not want option two in a plan designed for maximum retirement income: as you get older, your insurance costs increase. In option one, this is offset by the decreasing insurance that you are buying. But in option two, since the insurance remains the same over time, the cost of the insurance will increase. As a result, this option will cause you to have less money available for retirement income. This simple change in your policy could affect your income by over $10,000 per year. Over a ten-year retirement, option two could cost you $100,000 in comparison to the income that you would have had from the same policy without an increasing death benefit.

IF YOU DIE, YOU DO NOT GET YOUR MONEY

This is an argument that has been made against option one. And as you can see, that is not correct; your beneficiaries got your money, and the insurance company gave you less of theirs when you died. You were paying for less insurance, and your family was paid what you purchased, and the investment portion of your policy was paid, tax-free, to your beneficiaries. You can have option two if you'd like, but if you are using the IUL primarily for investment, you will get more income from your investment by using option one.

CHAPTER 10

CLOSING

KEEP YOUR EYE ON THE TARGET

I want to offer you this word of caution: do not abandon a long-term goal for a short-term need. These insurance products are long-term commitments. The longer you live and are participating in the product, the better the return you and your beneficiaries will get from your plan. That being said, I do understand that life often throws a grenade in our direction. We may need to adjust or modify our plan because our original path was blocked. I want to encourage you to never lose focus on what you are trying to achieve when these things happen in your life. Plan for these problems and understand how your plan can work for you when these events occur. If you understand how your plan can allow for changes in your life, then you won't abandon the mission as soon as you begin taking fire. Have a plan in place, and know that you are committed to it and to achieving your goal of the retirement that you deserve.

One of the most frustrating things that I experience in my career is when I work with a client who is are on their way and then, within the first couple of years, they abandon their plan due to a short-term need. I'm frustrated not because we will have to start over from scratch, but because I know that they have lost *time.* And as we've discussed, the time value of money is the biggest factor in any retirement equation.

Keep your eye on the target, even when you have a short-term issue. Have a plan in place. Contact your Quick Reaction Force (QRF) for directions on how to make sure that you can handle the short-term need without completely abandoning your long-term goals. Make sure that you plan for these things when you are putting together your retirement plan.

FIND AN AGENT

If this book was given to you by an agent that has met with you or is planning on meeting with you, they clearly have read it and understand the benefits of indexed products. Work with them on putting together a plan. Make sure that you discuss all your concerns and that your plan meets all your needs. Not all plans are alike from one company to the next, and plans can be designed and tailored to your needs. Make sure that your agent has taken all your needs into account and that you know how your plan will work for you under any contingency. With the information that you have been given in this book, you know what to look for, and you'll have a better understanding of the plan that they put together for you.

If you purchased this book in order to determine how to start your plan or how to protect the retirement savings that you have already put together, then now it is time to determine who will help you develop your plan. Who knows and can apply the principles taught in this book? Your agent should be someone that you can go to years into your plan, when life happens and you begin taking fire.

Your agent will be your QRF, the person that knows what your target is and the time horizon that you have determined to get there. Then, when your plan is being changed by life events, that agent needs to be there to help you determine how to modify your plan to compensate for the challenges that you're experiencing without getting you off the path. Your agent should know how to adjust your plan and keep you moving toward your target.

For those of you that purchased this book, I have established a network of qualified agents throughout the United States that understand what I have taught you. They are not part-time waiters, health insurance agents, or people that try to sell anything else. These are agents that sell investment-grade life insurance and know how to structure the plan for the maximum income potential. These are qualified agents that have been helping their clients put together their plans for years. In order to assist you in locating someone qualified who can help, you I have a contact form on my website, www.aprvbook.com. If you send us an agent location request, we will respond with the contact information for an agent in your area and pass your information on to them. If there is no one in your immediate area, we will let you know and try to set a telephone appointment with a qualified agent to get you started. You can also contact me directly through the website.

TAKE ACTION

The men and women of our armed forces are men and women of action. I challenge you to take what you have learned in this book and take action. Make changes! You now have the information you need to change your life and your future for you and your family. If these principles ring true and you feel that you know enough and are now empowered enough, begin planning. If you truly want to secure your financial independence, take the next step and contact someone who understands these principles and can help you achieve your retirement goals— someone who can provide you with a plan that you understand, believe in, and are committed to. With the right plan, you will be able to make your dreams a reality.

ENDNOTES

1   Forbes Magazine 8/21/2009 "The Compound Return Shell
    Game" authored by David Loeper

2   Forbes Magazine 8/21/2009 "The Compound Return Shell
    Game" authored by David Loeper

3   Google search "definition of inflation" 2nd listing (economics
    definition)

4   Bankers Life and Casualty Company Center for a Secure
    Retirement, Middle-Income Boomers, Financial Security
    and the New Retirement, 2011.

5   AARP 401(k) Participants' Awareness and Understanding of
    Fees Report July 2007. Section 1
    http://assets.aarp.org/rgcenter/econ/401k_fees.pdf

6   United States Department of Labor Publication "A Look at
    401(k) Plan Fees"
    http://www.dol.gov/ebsa/publications/401k_employee.
    html

7   Forbes Magazine 8/21/2009 "The Compound Return Shell
    Game" authored by David Loeper

8   www.401ksource.com ;

9   LIMRA 2012 Life Insurance Awareness Month Publication;
    http://www.limra.com/Posts/PR/LIAM/PDF/2012_Facts
    _of_Life_pdf.aspx

NOTES

NOTES

NOTES